First published in France under the title C'est dégoûtant!
© Editions du Seuil, 2001

English-language edition © 2003, 2011 by Black Dog & Leventhal Publishers, Inc.

Translated by Laura Ross

Black Dog & Leventhal Publishers
Hachette Book Group
1290 Avenue of the Americas
New York, NY 10104

www.hachettebookgroup.com
www.blackdogandleventhal.com

First Edition: February 2004

Black Dog & Leventhal Publishers is an imprint of Hachette Books, a division of Hachette Book Group. The Black Dog & Leventhal Publishers name and logo are trademarks of Hachette Book Group, Inc.

The publisher is not responsible for websites (or their content) that are not owned by the publisher.

The Hachette Speakers Bureau provides a wide range of authors for speaking events. To find out more, go to www.HachetteSpeakersBureau.com or call (866) 376-6591.

Library of Congress Control Number: 2004271422

ISBN: 978-1-57912-351-2

Printed in China

APS

20 19 18 17 16 15 14

THAT'S DISGUSTING!

Pittau   Gervais

BLACK DOG
& LEVENTHAL
PUBLISHERS
NEW YORK

Smelling a **sock**...

THAT's **DISGUSTING!**

Eating soap...

THAT'S **DISGUSTING!**

Sticking your hands in the jelly jar...

THAT'S **DISGUSTING!**

Rolling in the **mud** . . .

THAT'S **DISGUSTING!**

Drinking your **bath water**...

THAT'S DISGUSTING!

Sitting in **chocolate** . . .

THAT'S **DISGUSTING!**

Eating with your **hands**...

THAT'S **DISGUSTING!**

Letting slugs crawl down your **arms**...

THAT'S **DISGUSTING!**

Stepping in **dog poop**...

THAT'S DISGUSTING!

Sticking your finger in the **cat's behind** ...

THAT'S DISGUSTING!

Eating your **boogers**...

THAT'S **DISGUSTING!**

Finding a hair in your ice cream...

THAT'S **DISGUSTING!**

Never brushing your teeth...

THAT'S DISGUSTING!

Blowing your nose in your hands...

THAT's **DISGUSTING!**

Never taking a **bath**...

THAT'S DISGUSTING!

Getting covered with **flies**...

THAT'S DISGUSTING!

Blowing your nose on the **curtains**...

THAT'S DISGUSTING!

Brushing your teeth with paint...

THAT'S DISGUSTING!

Cutting your fingernails at the **table**...

THAT's DISGUSTING!

Stuffing your mouth with **hair**...

THAT's **DISGUSTING!**

Playing in the cat litter...

THAT'S DISGUSTING!

Getting bubblegum stuck in your hair...

THAT'S DISGUSTING!

Washing your feet in the **toilet**...

THAT'S **DISGUSTING!**

Getting **bird poop** on your head...

THAT'S **DISGUSTING!**

Sticking your head in a **garbage can**...

THAT's **DISGUSTING!**

Eating a lollipop covered with **sand**...

THAT'S DISGUSTING!

Combing your hair with a **toilet brush**...

THAT'S **DISGUSTING!**

Sticking boogers under your chair...

THAT'S **DISGUSTING!**

Pooping in the **bathtub**...

THAT's DISGUSTING!

Eating **worms**...

THAT'S **DISGUSTING!**

Swimming near a **sewer pipe**...

Painting with **ear wax**...

THAT's DISGUSTING!

Sculpting with cat poop...

THAT's DISGUSTING!

Throwing up at the **table**...

THAT'S **DISGUSTING!**

Reading this book...

THAT'S **DISGUSTING!**